STUDY GUIDE AND
PERSONAL REFLECTIONS

# Unshaken

### Sally Burke &
### Cyndie Claypool de Neve

D1456530

HARVEST HOUSE PUBLISHERS
EUGENE, OREGON

Cover by Connie Gabbert Design + Illustration

Published in association with William K. Jensen Literary Agency, 119 Bampton Court, Eugene, Oregon 97404.

**UNSHAKEN STUDY GUIDE AND PERSONAL REFLECTIONS**
Copyright © 2017 Sally Burke and Cyndie Claypool de Neve
Published by Harvest House Publishers
Eugene, Oregon 97402
www.harvesthousepublishers.com

ISBN 978-0-7369-6975-8 (pbk.)
ISBN 978-0-7369-6976-5 (eBook)

**Printed in the United States of America**

17 18 19 20 21 22 23 24 25 / VP-JC / 10 9 8 7 6 5 4 3 2 1

# Contents

I keep my eyes
*always on the Lord.*
With him at my right hand,
*I will not be shaken.*

Psalm 16:8

# His Strength to Remain Unshaken

We're excited to journey with you as we learn to stand unshaken in this shaken world. The news is dotted with terrorist attacks, school shootings, crime, horrific accidents, economic woes—so many reasons to make us frightened, worried, and filled with anxiety. Yet God didn't intend for us to live that way. He promises us His perfect peace when we hand over our worries to Him (Philippians 4:6-7).

As we travel this ten-week journey together, our guiding principle is found in Psalm 16:8: "I keep my eyes always on the LORD. With him at my right hand, I will not be shaken." This study guide is a companion to the book *Unshaken* and is designed to allow these prayer principles to burrow deep into your heart.

We've created lessons you can complete in a group study—or even alone—followed by five days of personal quiet-time prompts to deepen your prayer life and strengthen your relationship with the Lord. Sometimes studies can fill us with wonderful head knowledge from the Bible. But our goal is to help the truths of Scripture so penetrate our hearts and minds that we keep our eyes on the Lord and stand unshaken no matter what craziness tumbles around us.

You'll see in both the lessons and the quiet times that we've created expressive arts opportunities to help ensure the verses and important biblical truths don't stay only in our minds but also take root in our hearts. Sometimes you'll be asked to draw a picture; other times to artistically write a verse. In any case, please remember this is not about artistic abilities. Stick figures are great! The purpose is to help ingest God's truths in a way that can deeply affect our lives.

If you are journeying through this material with a group, you'll find resources in the last sections of this study guide to enrich that experience: Tips for Leading a Group; Group Prayer Time, which includes a sample schedule; and Praying in One Accord.

> This study was created using the New International Version of the Holy Bible. If you aren't sure what an answer for a fill-in space should be, please refer to an NIV version. In addition, sometimes the answers are indicated just below the question.

# 1

## Living Unshaken in a Shaken World

If we turn on the news—even for a couple of minutes—we have reason to feel shaken. Yet Philippians 4:4-7 tells us, "Rejoice in the Lord always. I will say it again: Rejoice! Let your gentleness be evident to all. The Lord is near. Do not be anxious about anything, but in every situation, by prayer and petition, with thanksgiving, present your requests to God. And the peace of God, which transcends all understanding, will guard your hearts and your minds in Christ Jesus."

Can we really have peace in this crazy world? Can we really be unshaken, standing firm on Christ Jesus, the rock of our salvation? Join us as we look at how we can use the four steps of prayer to help us stand unshaken, despite the craziness tumbling around us.

For each lesson, we encourage you to read the corresponding chapter in *Unshaken* first, before diving into the questions in this study guide. If you're going through the study with at least one other person, then after reading the chapter in the book, review the study guide lesson together, reading the text and sharing answers to the questions. Then, at the end of each lesson, are short reflection questions for five days a week. These are for you to use individually. To get the most out of each lesson, spend daily quiet time with God, asking, "Search me, God, and know my heart; test me and know my anxious thoughts" (Psalm 139:23).

Psalm 16:8 says, "I keep my eyes always on the LORD. With him at my right hand, I will not be shaken." To be able to really embrace this, we need to allow God to examine our hearts and show us our anxieties.

Let's start by looking at what causes us to be shaken, fearful, and anxious.

1. When do you feel the most stressed? Write or draw it below.

If you're going through this study in a group, share what you wrote or drew with at least one other person. (You might be surprised to find others have similar answers!)

2. Read Psalm 16:8-11 aloud.

> [8]I keep my eyes always on the LORD.
> With him at my right hand, I will not be shaken.
> [9]Therefore my heart is glad and my tongue rejoices;
> my body also will rest secure,
> [10]because you will not abandon me to the realm of the dead,
> nor will you let your faithful one see decay.
> [11]You make known to me the path of life;
> you will fill me with joy in your presence,
> with eternal pleasures at your right hand.

3. According to Psalm 16:8, whom do we need to focus on to be unshaken?

_____

4. To stand unshaken, how often do we need to keep our eyes on the Lord?

_____

5. What are some specific choices or activities that can help you keep your eyes on the Lord? Mark the ones you want to try this week.

☐ Read Scripture every day.

☐ Do the *Unshaken* quiet time for each of the five days.

☐ Take time to quietly pray throughout the day.

☐ Praise God often.

☐ Thank God specifically for His blessings throughout the day.

☐ Memorize scriptures.

☐ Listen to the Bible on CD during my commute.

☐ Listen to worship music.

☐ _____ (your own idea)

6. In verse 9, what are the benefits of keeping our eyes on the Lord, besides being unshaken?

"My heart is _____ and my tongue _____; my body also will _____ secure."

7. Isn't verse 9 a perfect example of God's peace? Illustrate that verse below. It doesn't need to be a nice piece of artwork. Stick figures are totally acceptable! The purpose of drawing is to help God's truths get deep into your heart and mind.

8. Now look at Philippians 4:4-9, which offers these commands with a promise:

> Rejoice in the Lord always. I will say it again: Rejoice! Let your gentleness be evident to all. The Lord is near. Do not be anxious about anything, but in every situation, by prayer and petition, with thanksgiving, present your requests to God. And the peace of God, which transcends all understanding, will guard your hearts and your minds in Christ Jesus. Finally, brothers and sisters, whatever is true, whatever is noble, whatever is right, whatever is pure, whatever is lovely, whatever is admirable—if anything is excellent or praiseworthy—think about such things. Whatever you have learned or received or heard from me, or seen in me—put it into practice. And the God of peace will be with you.

These words were written by Paul, whom God called from a life passionate about killing Christians to a life passionate about telling people about Christ and encouraging Christians in their personal walk with the Lord.

9. Share what you remember about Paul's life.

Even when he was shipwrecked, thrown in jail, or his life was threatened, Paul wasn't anxious or worried. He continued to rejoice, to be gentle, to pray, and to strive to maintain the mind of Christ. He poured out his heart to God in both petitions and thanksgiving. And what was the result? A peace mere humans cannot comprehend. Placing our faith and trust in our heavenly Father, allowing Him to be the blessed controller of our lives, results in a peaceful heart, free of worry: a heart that can stand resolute and unshaken.

10. What is your go-to stress reliever? Chocolate? Ice Cream? Exercise? Crafts? A girls' night out? Your favorite TV show? Your pet? Prayer? Re-reading a favorite Bible passage? List your top three.

11. Draw a picture of how you feel when you are *stressed*. (Again, stick figures are totally acceptable!)

12. Now draw a picture of yourself being *unshaken*, even with chaos swirling around you.

13. Think about the last stressful situation you endured (or maybe one you are in now). Which picture did you most look like—stressed or unshaken?

14. Now think back to a time when you felt completely overwhelmed and stressed. Do you think you would have reacted differently if you had been spending time praying and in the Word? Would you have felt unshaken? Why or why not?

15. Write a prayer to God, asking Him to help you in the area that feels the most stressful.

If you're in a group, depending on how much time you have left, break into twos and threes and spend time praying for each other using Psalm 16:8: "I keep my eyes always on the LORD. With him at my right hand, I will not be shaken." For example, "Lord, help Lisa set You before her, giving You the highest priority in her life so she will not be shaken."

Here's the verse with blanks for your prayer partner's name:

Lord, help _____ keep her eyes on You and have You at her right hand above all else, so _____ will not be shaken.

As time allows, stay in those small groups to pray for each other's biggest stressors.

# Personal Reflections

This first week, you'll use Psalm 16:8-11 to focus your time of prayer, marinating in and meditating on it. On the following pages you'll be guided through the four steps of prayer for five days.

A prayer on behalf of those pursuing a life unshaken in Christ:

> Dear Lord, we praise You that You are powerful and strong, as well as loving and compassionate. You are infinitely wise and sovereign, while also being a personal God. Forgive us for the times we take our eyes off You and begin to worry and fear, focusing more on our problems and not on You, our Problem Solver. We are so thankful for each one who has decided to embark on this life-changing study on prayer. You know what struggle each one is facing. Help us lift our eyes off our circumstances and focus instead on You so we can stand unshaken. Help these truths go deep into our hearts and minds. In the power of Your name, amen.

## Day One

Read Psalm 16:8-11 and then pray through the four steps of prayer as guided below.

## PRAISE

What attributes or descriptions of God's character stand out to you? Choose a different attribute each day.

## CONFESSION

Does anything in these verses bring to light some truth of sin in your own heart? What might you need to confess before the Lord who forgives?

## THANKSGIVING

In what way did God show Himself faithful to you yesterday or today?

## INTERCESSION

Whom do you know who needs God's strength and peace to be unshaken? Pray for them now, personalizing Psalm 16:8 by filling in the blank with the person's name.

Lord, help _____ keep his/her eyes on You and have You at his/her right hand above all else, so _____ will not be shaken.

## Day Two

Read Psalm 16:8-11 and then pray through the four steps of prayer as guided below.

## PRAISE

What attributes or descriptions of God's character stand out to you? Choose a different attribute each day.

## CONFESSION

Does anything in these verses bring to light some truth of sin in your own heart? What might you need to confess before the Lord who forgives?

## THANKSGIVING

In what way did God show Himself faithful to you yesterday or today? Thank God for specific times He carried you through.

## INTERCESSION

Whom do you know who needs God's strength and peace to be unshaken? Pray for them now, personalizing Psalm 16:8 by filling in the blank with the person's name.

Lord, help _____ keep his/her eyes on You and have You at his/her right hand above all else, so _____ will not be shaken.

# Day Three

Read Psalm 16:8-11 and then pray through the four steps of prayer as guided below.

## PRAISE

What attributes or descriptions of God's character stand out to you? Choose a different attribute each day.

## CONFESSION

Does anything in these verses bring to light some truth of sin in your own heart? What might you need to confess before the Lord who forgives?

## THANKSGIVING

In what way did God show Himself faithful to you yesterday or today? Thank God for specific times He carried you through.

## INTERCESSION

Whom do you know who needs God's strength and peace to be unshaken? Pray for them now, personalizing Psalm 16:8 by filling in the blank with the person's name.

Lord, help _____ keep his/her eyes on You and have You at his/her right hand above all else, so _____ will not be shaken.

# Day Four

Read Psalm 16:8-11 and then pray through the four steps of prayer as guided below.

## PRAISE

What attributes or descriptions of God's character stand out to you? Choose a different attribute each day.

## CONFESSION

Does anything in these verses bring to light some truth of sin in your own heart? What might you need to confess before the Lord who forgives?

## THANKSGIVING

In what way did God show Himself faithful to you yesterday or today? Thank God for specific times He carried you through.

## INTERCESSION

Whom do you know who needs God's strength and peace to be unshaken? Pray for them now, personalizing Psalm 16:8 by filling in the blank with the person's name.

Lord, help _____ keep his/her eyes on You and have You at his/her right hand above all else, so _____ will not be shaken.

## Day Five

Read Psalm 16:8-11 and then pray through the four steps of prayer as guided below.

## PRAISE

What attributes or descriptions of God's character stand out to you? Choose a different attribute each day.

## CONFESSION

Does anything in these verses bring to light some truth of sin in your own heart? What might you need to confess before the Lord who forgives?

## THANKSGIVING

In what way did God show Himself faithful to you yesterday or today? Thank God for specific times He carried you through.

## INTERCESSION

Whom do you know who needs God's strength and peace to be unshaken? Pray for them now, personalizing Psalm 16:8 by filling in the blank with the person's name.

Lord, help _____ keep his/her eyes on You and have You at his/her right hand above all else, so _____ will not be shaken.

# 2

# Experiencing the Power of Praise

As you read chapter 2 in *Unshaken*, you'll hear about real people who faced their terrifying problems by first praising God. These people are amazing examples of Colossians 3:2: "Set your minds on things above, not on earthly things." Each example is a real person with real emotions; yet in the midst of our trials we might dismiss those people as too dissimilar from us. Instead of thinking, "If they can do it, I can too," we think, "Well, if they were like me..." or "If they were in my shoes..." or even "There's no way I could face all those enemies [or the ridicule or the stress] like that."

But here's the thing—you can! Anyone can. Try this the next time you're starting to feel shaken: List all the amazing character traits and attributes of God. For example, He is compassionate, loving, forgiving, powerful, wise, our strength in our weakness, our provider, our finisher, our helper. He gives us wisdom, direction, peace, and protection. And the list goes on. By focusing on our all-powerful, all-loving heavenly Father, our earthly problems begin to feel smaller and less important. After all, there's not one problem God can't handle!

1. Paul wrote Colossians 3:1-2 while he was imprisoned.

   > Since, then, you have been raised with Christ, set your hearts on things above, where Christ is, seated at the right hand of God. Set your minds on things above, not on earthly things.

Underline the phrase Paul repeats twice, where he changes just one word.

What two words did he use in that phrase?

_____ and _____

2. What do you think the difference is between your heart and your mind?

3. What are we supposed to focus both on?

_____

4. Why do you think we're encouraged to set our hearts and minds on "things above"?

5. What do you think "things above" means?

6. How can focusing on God's character and attributes help you "set your mind [and hearts] on things above, not on earthly things"?

7. Read Psalm 46 aloud (even if you're alone). It's a great go-to passage when you're feeling overwhelmed, stressed, and totally shaken. As you read, write down each trait or attribute of God, such as "refuge" and "strength."

8. Write or draw your current stressful situation.

9. What character trait or attribute of God is most appealing to you given your current stress?

_____

10. Write a praise to God for that attribute. For example:

Lord, I praise You so much that You are an ever-present help in trouble. You know how difficult my situation is right now, and I praise You that You will help me through it—not just one time but continuously as "an ever-present help," giving me Your strength and being my refuge. Amen.

11. Look at Psalm 46:10. Besides praising Him, what does God tell us to do?

12. Close your eyes for a couple of minutes and begin to picture Psalm 46—being still in the midst of God's safe refuge, sitting at His feet while watching the streams from the river that "make glad the city of God."

Now illustrate what you just saw. It doesn't need to be a great drawing, just a reminder that in times of turmoil God is our "refuge and strength, an ever-present help in trouble." To allow this truth to settle deep in your heart, don't draw from your head knowledge; draw from your heart. Sometimes it's help-ful to use more "childlike" art supplies, like crayons, finger paints, or even Play-Doh. Pencils or pens are fine too.

Being still in the midst of turmoil can seem contrary to our human nature, but God reminds us He's going to take care of all the details, working them together for good (Romans 8:28).

13. Remember the story of Jehoshaphat from 2 Chronicles 20 we shared in chapter 2 of *Unshaken*? Jehoshaphat and his people were facing not one, but *three* armies. And what did he do? Verses 3 and 4 say,

> Alarmed, Jehoshaphat resolved to inquire of the LORD, and he pro-claimed a fast for all Judah. The people of Judah came together to seek

help from the LORD; indeed, they came from every town in Judah to seek him.

What did the people come together to do?

_____

14. Jehoshaphat began the prayer with praises to God and remembering His past miracles. Discuss (or write down) why you think it was important for him to start by praising God and not just dive into a list of prayer requests?

15. In verse 21, what did those at the front of the army say?

16. In verse 22, what was Jehoshaphat's army doing while the Lord was defeating the three armies who were coming to invade Judah?

17. Now take turns reading 2 Chronicles 20:25-30. In verse 25, what was the unexpected blessing God provided for His people?

18. In verse 26, in the midst of probable defeat and death, the people started by praising the Lord, trusting that God would defeat the three different armies coming to attack them. What did they do at the end of the conflict and blessing?

_____

19. Verse 27 says they returned _____ to Jerusalem, for the Lord had given them cause to _____ over their enemies.

20. Don't you just love verse 30? What happened at the end of the season of conflict? Jehoshaphat's entire kingdom was at _____, for his God had given him _____ on every side.

21. What character traits and attributes of God are illustrated in this amazing passage about Jehoshaphat?



22. Now write a praise to God. For example:

Lord, I praise You that You are ruler over all the kingdoms and nations, and that power and might are in Your hand. You alone give true deliverance. Like Jehoshaphat, I need only to look to You, because You will go before me and fight my battles. I praise You that You are our provider, and that You give us peace and rest. Amen.

23. If you're going through this study with a group, spend time praising God out loud, one attribute at a time, in one-accord prayer. Here's an example:

> **Person One:** Lord, we so praise You for being an ever-present help in trouble. You know I needed that reminder this week.
>
> **Person Two:** Yes, Lord, I, too, praise You for being our help, as well as being our refuge—a place where I can go to find Your peace and rest.
>
> **Person Three:** O heavenly Father, how I agree with these prayers. And I praise You that You are our provider, giving us more than what we need in Your perfect time.

Continue praying, one person at a time, with the leader closing in prayer.

## Personal Reflections

Each day this week read and meditate on Psalm 46. Spend time thinking through the questions presented for each of the five days.

A prayer on behalf of those pursuing a life unshaken in Christ:

> Lord, we praise You, our heavenly Creator, who loved each one of us so much that You came in human form to die on the cross as payment for our sins. We pray that our first response when we stumble will be to lift up our confession to You and to fix our eyes on You. We need only to trust You and follow Your guidance. Help us learn to praise You when we feel blessed and when we feel the storms of life swirling around us. Remind us of Psalm 16:11: "You make known to me the path of life; you will fill me with joy in your presence, with eternal pleasures at your right hand." Thank You for Your love and faithfulness. We ask for Your hand to guide those we care for so that they, too, can follow Your path of life. In Your precious name, amen.

## Day One

Read Psalm 46 and choose an attribute or character trait of God.

Attribute: _____

How does this attribute help you "be still" in relation to your concerns today?

Write or draw a praise to God for that attribute.

## Day Two

Read Psalm 46 again and choose a different attribute or character trait of God, as described in this lesson.

Attribute: _____

How does this attribute help you "be still" in relation to your concerns today?

Write or draw a praise to God for that attribute.

## Day Three

Read Psalm 46 again and choose a different attribute or character trait of God, as described in this lesson.

Attribute: _____

How does this attribute help you "be still" in relation to your concerns today?

Write or draw a praise to God for that attribute.

## Day Four

Read Psalm 46 again and choose a different attribute or character trait of God, as described in this lesson.

Attribute: _____

How does this attribute help you "be still" in relation to your concerns today?

Write or draw a praise to God for that attribute.

## Day Five

Read Psalm 46 again and choose a different attribute or character trait of God, as described in this lesson.

Attribute: _____

How does this attribute help you "be still" in relation to your concerns today?

Write or draw a praise to God for that attribute.

# 3

## Enabling God's Power Through Confession

Right about now, you might be saying to yourself, "The idea of being 'unshaken' during times of uncertainty and stress is admirable, but I don't think I can do this." And you're right! God knows that even as Christians, we need His help to live out a joy-filled and peace-filled life of Christlikeness. He desires that we reach out to Him in humility, acknowledging that we need His help. Philippians 4:13 says, "I can do all things through Him who strengthens me" (NASB).

1. Reflect on this past week. List the times you felt the most shaken. Maybe it was during a health or safety concern or during financial stress. Or because of school or work frustrations, family troubles, a family member's illness, or a horrifying news story.

2. Now look back at Philippians 4:13.

What can we do in God's strength?

_____

Yes, we can do "all"—*everything!*—through the power of Christ working in us!

And that includes confessing our fear, worry, frustration, anxiety, angst, and so on, so the peace only God gives can fill our hearts and minds.

3.  Did you know being anxious is a sin? Worry, fear, and anxiety prevent us from experiencing God's peace, which allows us to stand unshaken no matter life's circumstances. Philippians 4:6-7 says,

> Do not be anxious about anything, but in every situation, by prayer and petition, with thanksgiving, present your requests to God. And the peace of God, which transcends all understanding, will guard your hearts and your minds in Christ Jesus.

What does the peace of God do? _____ all understanding and _____ your hearts and your minds in Christ Jesus.

What does the peace of God guard? _____ Don't miss this point.

· · · · · · · · · · · · · · · · · · · · · · · · · · · · · ·

Confessing our anxiety to God is the key to being unshaken—to be filled with His inexplicable peace that stands guard around our hearts and minds during stressful and uncertain times. Romans 3:23 says, "For all have sinned and fall short of the glory of God." But each time we confess, we are washed clean. God promises to forgive our sins. First John 1:9 assures us, "If we confess our sins, he is faithful and just and will forgive us our sins and purify us from all unrighteousness."

Confession is a powerful weapon against the Enemy. By humbly coming to God and repenting of our sin—which He already knows about, anyway—we begin to release Satan's hold on our hearts and minds. This is different from the first time you acknowledge Jesus Christ is Lord. When you humbly accept Christ into your life as your Lord and Savior, that's it. You are part of His family for eternity.

If you're not sure if you have a relationship with God, know that your Creator is ready with open arms to accept you into His family. Salvation is a *free* gift, and only requires that you ask forgiveness of your sins and invite Jesus into your life as your Lord and Savior. Romans 10:9 says, "If you declare with your mouth, 'Jesus is Lord,' and believe in your heart that God raised him from the dead, you will be saved." You can pray a simple prayer like this:

> Lord, I have sinned and fallen short of God's standard. But I believe Jesus died for my sins on the cross and that He was raised again on the third day according to Scripture. Please come into my life and be my Lord and Savior. Thank You that I now belong to You and Your family, and that no one can snatch me out of my Father's hand.

If you prayed this prayer, *welcome to the family!*

4. Even after we ask Christ to be Lord of our lives, we have to be on guard. The Enemy strives to take our eyes off the Lord. Sin will impede our relationship with Him, and unconfessed sin will cause built-up guilt that will drive a wedge between us and our Savior—and between us and others in our lives. Satan draws us to sin the same way he did back in the garden of Eden—through the lust of the eyes, the lust of the flesh, and the pride of life. Yet when Christ died for our sins, He died for all our sins, including the penalty and the suffocating bondage sin holds.

Romans 3:23-25 (NLT) says,

> For everyone has sinned; we all fall short of God's glorious standard. Yet God, in his grace, freely makes us right in his sight. He did this through Christ Jesus when he freed us from the penalty for our sins. For God presented Jesus as the sacrifice for sin. People are made right with God when they believe that Jesus sacrificed his life, shedding his blood.

How many of us sin?

_____

When we sin, whose standard do we fall short of?

_____

How can we be made right in God's sight?

_____

. . . . . . . . . . . . . . . . . . . . . . . . . . . .

The act of confessing includes three parts: admitting we've sinned, asking for God's forgiveness, and then turning away from the sin. Whenever we sin, no matter how small or large that transgression is, we must confess it to God and turn away from it, so we don't squelch the Holy Spirit in our lives.

We want that peace that surpasses all understanding to guard our hearts and minds in Christ Jesus. We want that peace to rule our hearts! We want God's inexplicable joy found in Him no matter the circumstances. We want His infinite, unconditional love and power to flow through us to others. We want to fulfill the great calling He has on our lives. And we want to bring Him glory and live a life pleasing to Him.

Yet the Enemy will do anything he can to stop you by trying to entangle you in sin. Don't let him!

5. Read Hebrews 12:1-3. What can easily entangle us? _____
Whom do we fix our eyes on so we don't get entangled by sin or distracted by things that hinder us? _____

6. Think back to the previous lessons. Why is it important that we are "fixing our eyes on Jesus, the pioneer and perfecter of faith"?

......................................

The first step in confession is the hardest—acknowledging the sin. We don't want to acknowledge it because it makes us feel bad. But once we let God reveal it to us, He can give us the strength to conquer it. And, oh—the sweet refreshment of confessing to God and restoring our relationship with God Almighty.

Do you want to stand unshaken? You must ask God to search your heart and confess your sin to your loving heavenly Father. Then He can fill you with His peace and joy to overflowing.

7. Psalm 51:10 says, "Create in me a pure heart, O God, and renew a steadfast spirit within me." What does David want God to create in him?

_____

Remember, only God can cleanse our hearts. In this verse, the word *create* is translated from the Hebrew word *bara*, which means to make something new out of nothing.

What does David ask to have *renewed*?

_____

What does "renew" imply?

_____

8. Two verses later, in Psalm 51:12, David also asks God, "Restore to me the joy of your salvation." In Psalm 51:10 and 12, after David confesses and asks God to cleanse him and give him a pure heart, what does David anticipate having renewed and restored?

David is a great example of coming to God with a "contrite heart," as he said in verse 17, expecting that God will forgive him and cleanse his heart. His goal? To have a renewed, steadfast spirit and be filled again with the joy of salvation.

9. Read Psalm 32.

In verses 3 and 4, what is described as happening when we try to keep sin unconfessed?

In verse 5, what does David say happens after he acknowledges and confesses his sin?

10. Meditate on and pray through Psalm 139:23-24 to God. "Search me, God, and know my heart; test me and know my anxious thoughts. See if there is any offensive way in me, and lead me in the way everlasting."

On the provided blank page, draw a cross. Then pray alone with God, asking Him to reveal to you any sins you need to confess. As God reveals various sins in your life, write them on the paper around the cross. Spend time confessing, asking God to forgive each one of those sins and humbly asking Him to help you be strong against temptation whenever opportunity arises.

When you're finished, tear out the sheet with your sins listed on it and tear it into tiny pieces. If possible, throw the pieces away in as many trash cans as you can find, to remind yourself of the truth found in Psalm 103:12: "As far as the east is from the west, so far has he removed our transgressions from us." Micah 7:19 talks about God hurling "all our iniquities [sins] into the depths of the sea"—so don't go fishing for them!

Spend time thanking your Holy Father for forgiving your sins.

# Take Your Sin to the Cross

As far as
the *east* is from the *west,*
so far has he
*removed our
transgressions from us.*

Psalm 103:12

# Personal Reflections

During this week's reflections and times with the Lord, keep in mind the three parts of confession: admitting we sinned, asking for God's forgiveness, and turning away from the sin. Each day's meditation will help you follow through with one, two, or all three of these steps of confession.

A prayer on behalf of those pursuing a life unshaken in Christ:

Lord, You know all that is in our hearts. We praise You for seeing and knowing us as a loving heavenly Father. Show us what sins we need to confess before You so we can clear our communication channel with You. You tell us not to fear or be anxious. Please forgive us for each time we take our eyes off You and instead focus on our doubt, fear, and worry, allowing our concerns to consume our minds and hearts. O Lord, we pray You will help us let go of our sin, especially the sin we cling to. Thank You for the promise that if we confess our sins to You, You are faithful and just to forgive us our sins and purify us from all unrighteousness. We pray that You will indeed cleanse our hearts and purify us so we will be clean vessels before You, able to be filled with the fruit of the Holy Spirit. Help every woman longing to remain unshaken seek to be a pure vessel so Your work, love, and grace will flow through her. Bless us as we seek to maintain a strong walk with You. In Your name we pray, amen.

## Day One

Meditate on Philippians 4:6-7.

> Do not be anxious about anything, but in every situation, by prayer and petition, with thanksgiving, present your requests to God. And the peace of God, which transcends all understanding, will guard your hearts and your minds in Christ Jesus.

In what circumstances are you most anxious? Write or draw them here.

Now write a prayer to God giving Him those worries and asking Him to replace those worries with His peace that guards our hearts and minds in Christ Jesus.

## Day Two

Meditate on Psalm 103:10-14.

> He does not treat us as our sins deserve or repay us according to our iniquities. For as high as the heavens are above the earth, so great is his love for those who fear him; as far as the east is from the west, so far has he removed our transgressions [sin] from us. As a father has compassion on his children, so the Lord has compassion on those who fear him; for he knows how we are formed, he remembers that we are dust.

In the passage above, circle any words or phrases that describe our heavenly Father and then write a praise to God for who He is.

## Day Three

Meditate on 1 John 1:8-10.

> If we claim to be without sin, we deceive ourselves and the truth is not in us. If we confess our sins, he is faithful and just and will forgive us our sins and purify us from all unrighteousness. If we claim we have not sinned, we make him out to be a liar and his word is not in us.

Ask God to show you any areas where you might be deceiving yourself about sin in your life. Confess that sin to God so He can cleanse you completely.

## Day Four

Meditate on James 4:1-3.

> What causes fights and quarrels among you? Don't they come from your desires that battle within you? You desire but do not have, so you kill. You covet but you cannot get what you want, so you quarrel and fight. You do not have because you do not ask God. When you ask, you do not receive, because you ask with wrong motives, that you may spend what you get on your pleasures.

Are you fighting or quarreling with someone? Ask God to reveal the source of the quarrel. Then pray that He'll help you humble your heart and see how to resolve this conflict with right motives.

## Day Five

In Psalm 15, we are told, "Whoever does these things will never be shaken" (verse 5). Read Psalm 15 in your Bible or Bible app as a way to inspect your heart. Is God convicting you of anything in this passage? Circle it or write it down. Then write a prayer below, asking God to forgive you and to help you not continue in that sin.

Sit quietly before the Lord and ask Him if He needs to clean out anything else in your heart before you can experience His peace. Write or draw anything additional God brings to your mind.

# 4

# Transforming the Dark Through Thanksgiving

Around the world, in more than 140 countries, women gather in groups to pray for their children and schools. Imagine what these moms go through: abductions, wars, terrorist attacks, oppression from governments who want to eradicate Christianity, danger from drug lords ruling the community—not to mention concerns about bullying, drug abuse, gangs, sexual behavior, learning disabilities, education, their children's futures, and so on. The more we focus on these things, the more the list of fears and concerns will grow.

Yet the women who gather weekly to pray leave the "hour of power" filled with hope, peace, and confidence in Christ. Each group starts with praising God, as we talked about in the first lesson. Not only is this modeled in Scripture, but it's the very best way to shift our focus from the problem onto the Problem Solver. Second, we silently confess our sins, asking God to cleanse our hearts and minds to prepare to hear the Holy Spirit as we pray for our children and their schools. Is it time to pray our requests now? No, there's a third step before we ever get to prayer requests.

Do you remember what the third step of prayer is?

_____

1. We looked at Philippians 4 previously, but let's review Philippians 4:4-7. How are we supposed to present our requests to God? "With _____."

God commands us, over and over again, to be thankful and to remember what He has done. This isn't just remembering who God is and what He's capable of, like we focus on during praise time. This is thanking God for specific ways He's answered prayers or has done "more than all we ask or imagine," as it says in Ephesians 3:20.

2. Why do you think it's important to offer thanksgiving for what God has done before we begin to pray?

3. Psalm 78:4-7 urges us to share the testimonies of thanksgivings to the next generation. Read this passage out loud (even if you're alone). Why do you think it's important to share answers to prayer with others?

• • • • • • • • • • • • • • • • • • • • • • • • • • •

Spending time being thankful reminds us of the specific ways our heavenly Father has answered our prayers in the past. And because He has answered our prayers before, it reminds us to ask big and bold requests of Him, so we can experience the "Holy Spirit party" of thanksgiving, again and again. This increases our faith. We witness the names, attributes, and character of God come alive through answered prayer.

4. Write a list of ten things for which you're thankful.

1.

2.

3.

4.

5.

6.

7.

8.

9.

10.

Star any of those items that were answers to specific prayer requests.

5. Now write a prayer of thanksgiving to God for those answered prayers.

. . . . . . . . . . . . . . . . . . . . . . . . . .

If you're going through this study as a group, spend time thanking God for His blessings and answered prayers. We suggest using the one-accord prayer method, focusing on one thanksgiving at a time, and allowing at least one other person to also thank God for each answer to prayer.

**Person One:** Lord, I thank You that You handpicked the exact teacher my child needed. It has been so exciting to see her flourish under Mr. Johnson's guidance. This was such a huge answer to prayer, and I thank You.

**Person Two:** Lord, I so agree! Thank You for putting Michelle in this class where she is learning and growing in confidence. I also thank You for protecting their school campus. Despite all the flooding around town, the staff was able keep each child safe while at school and during pickup. Thank You for loving and caring for each of those children and for giving the school staff wisdom and foresight.

**Person Three:** Lord, we thank You for the specific ways You provide for our children!

## Now it's time to pray!

6. When you've spent time thanking the Lord, share how you feel after giving thanks and hearing others' thanksgivings. Write some of those feelings and insights here.

7. God doesn't tell us to thank Him only for the good things and answered prayers. Check out 1 Thessalonians 5:16-18: "Rejoice always, pray continually, give thanks in all circumstances; for this is God's will for you in Christ Jesus." In what circumstances are we supposed to give thanks?

8. In what circumstance or difficulty is it hardest for you to give thanks? Draw or write an explanation of that situation.

9. Do you have Romans 8:28 memorized? If so, recite it. Then look up the verse in the Bible. How might God be working out the difficulties in your life right now for good, as Romans 8:28 says?

10. Take a minute to pray and ask God to help you be thankful for this difficult situation.

Now write a thanksgiving to God for that situation. It could be something like this:

Lord, I thank You for carrying me through this painful time. Thank You that I can trust that You will work everything together for good because I love You and am called according to Your good purpose, as You tell us in Romans 8:28 and Ephesians 2:10. Thank You that Your Holy Spirit is working in me and will give me the strength and wisdom to persevere. Amen.

11. Was it hard to be thankful for this difficulty?

12. How did you feel *after* you thanked God for the difficulty?

13. Read Colossians 3:15. "Let the peace of Christ rule in your hearts, since as members of one body you were called to peace. And be thankful." What does this verse mean to you?

14. How does letting God's peace rule in our hearts help us be more thankful?

15. Paul wrote Colossians while he was imprisoned for his faith, yet he mentions being thankful several times. Colossians 3:17 says, "And whatever you do, whether in word or deed, do it all in the name of the Lord Jesus, giving thanks to God the Father through him." How can being thankful help us do everything in the name of Jesus Christ?

16. Read Colossians 4:2. What are we to devote ourselves to?

_____

And how are we to devote ourselves to prayer?

By being_____ and _____.

17. What do you think being "watchful" has to do with being thankful?

. . . . . . . . . . . . . . . . . . . . . . . . . . . .

When you're focused on prayer and looking for ways God is working out His good purpose, then your heart rests peacefully in Christ Jesus. A thankful heart pushes away the frustrations and anxieties of life and helps you to "set your mind[s] on things above, not on earthly things," as it says in Colossians 3:2.

As we thank Him in the midst of our struggles, we begin to see past our current circumstances and stand unshaken. Then we're able to respond to people and situations with God's love and wisdom.

18. Finish today's lesson by creating a drawing of you being devoted to prayer, being watchful and thankful as it says in Colossians 4:2. (Remember, there are no bonus points for artistic abilities! This is an expression between you and God to help you remember to be devoted to prayer, being watchful and thankful.)

# Personal Reflections

Having a thankful heart is a matter of shifting focus from the problem to the Problem Solver. To do that, we need to bathe our minds and hearts in Scripture. This week you'll have verses to meditate on, reading them over and over, and then you'll illustrate those verses by writing them out artistically or by drawing pictures of you following the commands of the verses. Also, each day, list seven different items for which you're thankful. Choose new ones each day.

A prayer on behalf of those pursuing life unshaken in Christ:

Lord, we praise You for Your loving presence, and that You are always with us. You give us Your joy and peace to overflowing no matter the chaos that swirls around us. You tell us to be thankful in all circumstances—but this can be so difficult. Forgive us when we doubt our power in Christ. In the midst of painful or scary times, we need Your enduring strength and wisdom to show us how to be thankful, how to move our eyes from our problems to You, the Problem Solver. As we strive this week to have thankful hearts, transform our minds from agony to joy, from fear to boldness, from negativity to thankfulness. Instill in those around us a deep passion to also be transformed. And give us all the deep longing for the Holy Spirit to fill us with Your joy and peace. In the name of our Savior Jesus Christ, amen.

## Day One

List seven things for which you are thankful.

1.

2.

3.

4.

5.

6.

7.

Illustrate or artistically write 1 Thessalonians 5:16-18: "Rejoice always, pray continually, give thanks in all circumstances; for this is God's will for you in Christ Jesus."

## Day Two

List seven things for which you are thankful.

1.

2.

3.

4.

5.

6.

7.

Illustrate or artistically write Colossians 3:15: "Let the peace of Christ rule in your hearts, since as members of one body you were called to peace. And be thankful."

# Day Three

List seven things for which you are thankful.

1.

2.

3.

4.

5.

6.

7.

Illustrate or artistically write Colossians 3:17: "And whatever you do, whether in word or deed, do it all in the name of the Lord Jesus, giving thanks to God the Father through him."

## Day Four

List seven things for which you are thankful.

1.

2.

3.

4.

5.

6.

7.

Illustrate or artistically write Romans 8:28: "And we know that in all things God works for the good of those who love him, who have been called according to his purpose."

## Day Five

List seven things for which you are thankful.

1.

2.

3.

4.

5.

6.

7.

Illustrate or artistically write Philippians 4:6-7:

> Rejoice in the Lord always. I will say it again: Rejoice! Let your gentleness be evident to all. The Lord is near. Do not be anxious about anything, but in every situation, by prayer and petition, with thanksgiving, present your requests to God. And the peace of God, which transcends all understanding, will guard your hearts and your minds in Christ Jesus.

# 5

# Wielding the Secret Weapon of Intercession

We have journeyed through an understanding of the first three steps of prayer. It is such a gift to draw closer to God's heart and to feel His presence more deeply. The more frequently you pray the four steps of prayer, the more quickly your heart will turn toward God in every situation and circumstance. This will change your life, your family, and your future.

1. How did your attitude change last week when you were focused on giving thanks to God?

2. Share one of your favorite answers to prayer, whether recent or in the past. If you're new to prayer, choose an answer to prayer highlighted in the book *Unshaken*.

3. Read 1 John 5:14-15. What prayers does God hear?

That if we ask _____ according to God's _____ .
Looking at these verses, why do you think we spend time preparing our hearts
for prayer before we begin praying for our requests?

4.  Do you remember what the first step of prayer is?

_____

Do you want to be able to pray according to God's will? Then it's important
to first remember that God is Almighty, the Creator, our loving Savior, our
strength in our weakness, our peace, our joy, and so on. Once we start remembering with whom we are communicating, we're ready for the next step.

5.  Do you remember what the second step of prayer is?

_____

Confession is asking God to search our hearts, then humbly confessing the sin
He shows us, and repenting, asking His help to not commit the sin again. This
kind of confession is like cleaning out a gunky water pipe so the clear water can
flow smoothly again. When we confess and cleanse our hearts, we don't stifle
the Holy Spirit, and we're able to hear God's leading in our prayers.

6.  Do you remember what the third step is?

_____

After confession, we spend time celebrating the answers to prayer that God has
provided. And then after praise, confession, and thanksgiving comes the fourth
step: intercession.

7. What do you think "intercession" means?

This is the time when we pray for others, asking God to move mightily in someone's life. And, boy, does He! Think of "intercede" like "intersect." When we intercede in prayer on someone else's behalf, we invite God into his or her life. Often, the answer to prayer becomes like an intersection, where God can change the direction of a life through the answered prayer.

8. Why, if you want to remain unshaken, do you think it's important not to dive straight into prayer requests?

By starting with praise, confession, and thanksgiving and not just diving into requests, we grow our faith. We're reminded what a big God we serve and how often our problems are small in comparison. Sometimes, by preparing our hearts first and shifting our eyes from the problem onto God, our prayer requests change. We might pray more specifically or pray with a bigger picture in mind.

9. Read James 5:16-18.

> Therefore confess your sins to each other and pray for each other so that you may be healed. The prayer of a righteous person is powerful and effective. Elijah was a human being, even as we are. He prayed earnestly that it would not rain, and it did not rain on the land for three and a half years. Again he prayed, and the heavens gave rain, and the earth produced its crops.

How does this passage describe Elijah, a great prophet of God?

Elijah was a _____ , even as_____ .

10. In the selection from James, underline the words "confess your sins"; "he prayed earnestly"; and "the prayer of a righteous person is powerful and effective." Looking at the words you underlined, why do you think God answered Elijah's big and bold prayers?

11. What can we do so God will answer our big and bold prayers?

When we confess and repent of our sins, we clear our channel with God so we can more clearly hear His will as we pray. Then we should pray "earnestly"—intently, with conviction—believing that God will answer our prayers.

· · · · · · · · · · · · · · · · · · · · · · · · · · ·

In Matthew 17, the disciples asked Christ why they couldn't heal a child. His answer:

> Because you have so little faith. Truly I tell you, if you have faith as small as a mustard seed, you can say to this mountain, "Move from here to there," and it will move. Nothing will be impossible for you (Matthew 17:20).

Our faith is in the Creator of the entire universe. Nothing is too hard or impossible for Him! Of course, God's will is not that we each have an easy life. Often it's through our struggles that we become more Christlike. But if we have prepared for intercession through praise, confession, and thanksgiving, then we're ready to pray earnestly for someone in need, guided by the Holy Spirit.

Are you ready to intercede in prayer for someone?

If you're going through this study alone, you can journal your prayers. If you're with a group, pray the first three steps together: praise, silent confession, and thanksgiving. Then spend a couple of minutes in silent prayer, asking the Lord for whom you should pray. This could be a family member, a friend, or just someone you know who needs prayer. Then break into groups of two or three, with each woman leading out prayer for someone in her life. As was illustrated in the previous lesson and in the Praying in One Accord section in the back, pray in one accord with the prayer partners also praying for that person. No discussion is needed. Just pray the request, and the prayer partners will then each take turns praying for that request. Pray back and forth until you've covered that person in prayer.

Now let's pray.

## Personal Reflections

This week you will pray through the four steps of prayer each day, focusing on a person or several people who you want to intercede for in prayer. Take time to think about who God is placing on your heart or in your life to pray for specifically.

A prayer on behalf of those pursuing a life unshaken in Christ:

> Lord, what an amazing privilege You've given us to intercede in prayer in the lives of others. Open our eyes to see the needs around us so we can pray powerfully for others and make an impact on the world for Christ through intercessory prayer. Give us Your eyes to see the heartaches, anxiety, and

deep concerns of those around us so we can bring those needs to You. Draw us close to You as we pray boldly and confidently. And, Lord, we pray that our faith will grow stronger and stronger as we witness You move mightily as a result of our prayers. In Your powerful name, amen.

## Day One

Read 2 Samuel 22:2-4.

Write a prayer of praise.

Write a prayer of confession.

Write a prayer of thanksgiving.

Sit quietly and ask God for whom you should intercede. Then write a prayer of intercession for that person.

## Day Two

Read Psalm 33:1-4.

Write a prayer of praise.

Write a prayer of confession.

Write a prayer of thanksgiving.

Sit quietly and ask God for whom you should intercede. Then write a prayer of intercession for that person.

# Day Three

Read Psalm 30:11-12.

Write a prayer of praise.

Write a prayer of confession.

Write a prayer of thanksgiving.

Sit quietly and ask God for whom you should intercede. Then write a prayer of intercession for that person.

# Day Four

Psalm 40:1-3.

Write a prayer of praise.

Write a prayer of confession.

Write a prayer of thanksgiving.

Sit quietly and ask God for whom you should intercede. Then write a prayer of intercession for that person.

# Day Five

Read Psalm 100:1-5.

Write a prayer of praise.

Write a prayer of confession.

Write a prayer of thanksgiving.

Sit quietly and ask God for whom you should intercede. Then write a prayer of intercession for that person.

# 6

## Praying God's Words Back to Him

Remember 1 John 5:14-15, which we looked at last week. "This is the confidence we have in approaching God: that if we ask anything according to his will, he hears us. And if we know that he hears us—whatever we ask—we know that we have what we asked of him."

1. Use colored pencils, pens, or crayons to handwrite the above verse, emphasizing the most important words in a big and bold way.

2. What is the key to asking for a request in a way that God not only hears but answers with a resounding "yes"? "If we ask anything according to _____ ." Did you catch that? If we ask requests that align with God's will, He will grant us that request!

It can be difficult to know how to pray God's will, especially if it's for ourselves or someone we're close to. We more often pray *our desire* instead of *God's will*. Say you pray fervently that your daughter gets in a specific school or class. Yet God doesn't make that happen. Instead she ends up in a class with a teacher who is adamantly opposed to Christ, and she doesn't have any of her friends from church in that class.

Is it possible that God is working out the very best plan in your child's life? Is it possible that she might learn life lessons she would never have learned in a class with her church friends? And perhaps the teacher needs a friendly, helpful Christian in her life to be a nonjudgmental example of Christ's love. To top that off, you'll have a whole new class of students to pray for—and chances are they need the prayers more than you can imagine.

3.  How do you think we can pray in a way we know is God's will?

When we pray God's own words back to Him, we can be assured we are praying His will. Isaiah 55 tells us God's words never return empty.

4.  Read Hebrews 4:12 and underline each description of God's Word.

> For the word of God is alive and active. Sharper than any double-edged sword, it penetrates even to dividing soul and spirit, joints and marrow; it judges the thoughts and attitudes of the heart.

5.  Now read 2 Timothy 3:16-17. "All Scripture is God-breathed and is useful for teaching, rebuking, correcting and training in righteousness, so that the servant of God may be thoroughly equipped for every good work."

What is Scripture useful for?


What is the goal of the Scripture, beautifully described as "God-breathed"?


........................................

Imagine if we focused our prayers for our loved ones on scripture that teaches, rebukes, corrects, and trains in righteousness, so that they will be completely ready for every good work God puts in their paths. Wow, how God could transform their lives!

Are you ready to intercede for others through transformational scripture prayers? We will give you some scripture prayers here, and we have several listed in the book *Unshaken*. However, as you read your Bible, you can find powerful verses on your own and then begin to pray it for your family members, friends, and loved ones.

6. Let's start with Romans 12:2. Here's the verse: "Do not conform to the pattern of this world, but be transformed by the renewing of your mind. Then you will be able to test and approve what God's will is—his good, pleasing and perfect will." Using this verse, write a prayer for a friend or loved one.

•••••••••••••••••••••••••••••

Here's how you could pray this same verse in Romans in one-accord, agreement prayer with one or two prayer partners:

> **Person One:** Lord, help Kassandra not be conformed to the pattern of this world, but help her be transformed by the renewing of her mind. Guide her in being able to test and approve what Your will is, Your good, pleasing, and perfect will.
>
> **Person Two:** Lord, we agree with that prayer. Give her Your strength and confidence to be able to stand up against temptation and help her to know what Your good, pleasing, and perfect will is.
>
> **Person One or Three:** Yes, Lord, and I pray that the Holy Spirit will completely transform her mind, so that she has the mind of Christ.

When you have covered that person in prayer, another person prays the scripture prayer for someone else, with the other(s) praying in one-accord, agreement prayer.

## Praying Scripture Prayers

Let's spend time praying scripture prayers. To start, here's a list of verses to pray for others. We've added a blank where you can fill in a name.

If you are in a group, again practice praising God in one-accord, agreement prayer. (Refer to the Praying in One Accord section at the back of the book.) Then have a time of silent confession, followed by an opportunity to thank God for answered prayers as well as His blessings. Then sit quietly and ask Him for whom you should pray.

Break into groups of twos or threes and pray the following scriptures for people in your lives. Pray one verse and for one person at a time, with the others adding onto the prayer as the Holy Spirit leads. Once you've thoroughly prayed the verse for that one person, the next person in the group chooses a verse and prays for the loved one, with the prayer partner(s) praying in one-accord, agreement prayer. Go back and forth until you feel that person has been covered in prayer.

Start with the following verse. Then choose additional verses as you have time.

## Romans 12:2

Lord, help _____ not conform to the pattern of this world, but be transformed by the renewing of her mind. Guide _____ in being able to test and approve what Your will is—Your good, pleasing, and perfect will.

## Additional Scripture Prayers

## Proverbs 3:5-6

Lord, help_____ trust in You with all his heart and lean not on his own understanding. In all his ways help _____ submit to You, so You will make his paths straight.

## Ephesians 3:16-21

I pray that out of Your glorious riches, You strengthen _____ with power through Your Spirit in her inner being, so that Christ may dwell in her heart through faith. And I pray that _____ will be rooted and established in Your love, so that she may have power, together with all the Lord's holy people, to grasp how wide and long and high and deep is the love of Christ, and to know this love that surpasses knowledge—that _____ may be filled to the measure of all the fullness of God.

## Ephesians 1:17-18

I keep asking You, our Lord Jesus Christ, the glorious Father, to give _____ the Spirit of wisdom and revelation, so that he may know You better. I pray that the eyes of _____ 's heart may be enlightened so that he may know the hope to which You have called him, the riches of Your glorious inheritance in Your holy people.

## Isaiah 40:31

Lord, help _____ hope in the Lord and renew her strength. Help her soar on wings like eagles; help _____ run and not grow weary, walk and not be faint.

## Psalm 16:8

Help _____ keep his eyes always on the Lord, so that with You at _____ 's right hand, he will not be shaken.

# Personal Reflections

This week pray through the four steps of prayer. During the intercession time, start by praying the scripture for the person for whom you're praying.

A prayer on behalf of those pursuing life unshaken in Christ:

Lord, You tell us Your Word does not come back void but fulfills Your purposes. Teach us that the power of Your word combined with intercessory prayer can move mountains in people's lives in Your perfect timing. Give us a passion for Your holy Word, so that scriptures will take root in our hearts and blossom into prayers as soon as we hear a need. May Scripture so reside in our hearts and minds that our first response to any event that has us feeling shaken is to pray Your Word back to You. Use us to change the world by praying Your Word and will into the lives and circumstances around us. In the strength of Your name, amen.

## Day One

Write a prayer of praise.

Write a prayer of confession.

Write a prayer of thanksgiving.

Sit quietly and ask God for whom you should intercede, using Romans 12:2.

Lord, help _____ not conform to the pattern of this world, but be transformed by the renewing of her mind. Guide _____ in being able to test and approve what Your will is—Your good, pleasing, and perfect will.

# Day Two

Write a prayer of praise.

Write a prayer of confession.

Write a prayer of thanksgiving.

Sit quietly and ask God for whom you should intercede, using Proverbs 3:5-6.

Lord, help _____ trust in You with all his heart and lean not on his own understanding. In all his ways help _____ submit to You, so You will make his paths straight.

# Day Three

Write a prayer of praise.

Write a prayer of confession.

Write a prayer of thanksgiving.

Sit quietly and ask God for whom you should intercede, using Ephesians 3:16-21.

I pray that out of Your glorious riches, You strengthen _____ with power through Your Spirit in her inner being, so that Christ may dwell in her heart through faith. And I pray that _____ will be rooted and established in Your love, so that she may have power, together with all the Lord's holy people, to grasp how wide and long and high and deep is the love of Christ, and to know this love that surpasses knowledge—that _____ may be filled to the measure of all the fullness of God.

# Day Four

Write a prayer of praise.

Write a prayer of confession.

Write a prayer of thanksgiving.

Sit quietly and ask God for whom you should intercede, using Isaiah 40:31.

> Lord, help _____ hope in You and renew his strength. Help him soar on wings like eagles; help _____ run and not grow weary, walk and not be faint.

# Day Five

Write a prayer of praise.

Write a prayer of confession.

Write a prayer of thanksgiving.

Sit quietly and ask God for whom you should intercede, using Psalm 16:8.

> Help _____ keep her eyes always on the Lord, so that, with You at _____'s right hand, she will not be shaken.

# 7

## Petitioning on Your Own Behalf

It's often hard to pray God's will for our own lives because we're pretty opinionated about the direction our lives should go. We know what we want, and what we do *not* want, so it can be difficult to remember God's promise to work all things together for good (Romans 8:28) when we're in the middle of a stressful situation. Yet that very hope will help propel us forward in peace and thankfulness, standing unshaken in a shaky time.

1. Do you find it easy or hard to pray for yourself? Why?

2. When you pray for yourself, what are some of your typical prayer requests?

3. Think back a few lessons. What do we need to focus on to remain unshaken?

---

If you answered Christ, you are correct!

4. In the space below, illustrate John 15:5-8, one verse at a time. You can build upon the same picture or create separate pictures. Remember, this is not about drawing abilities. The expressive arts help us move God's truths from head knowledge to our heart. Read John 15:5-8, pausing after each individual verse to draw your interpretation of the verse.

> [5] I am the vine; you are the branches. If you remain in me and I in you, you will bear much fruit; apart from me you can do nothing. [6] If you do not remain in me, you are like a branch that is thrown away and withers; such branches are picked up, thrown into the fire and burned. [7] If you remain in me and my words remain in you, ask whatever you wish, and it will be done for you. [8] This is to my Father's glory, that you bear much fruit, showing yourselves to be my disciples.

5. What is the promise in verse 7?

_____

In verse 7, Jesus says, "Ask whatever you wish, and it will be done for you."

6. What do you have to do for God to answer your prayers with a yes?

7. Look back up to verses 5 and 6. Why do you think Jesus uses the illustration of a vine and a branch to explain this principle?

8. Why, as we're told in verse 8, does God answer our prayers and allow us to bear fruit?

9. In lesson 8, we discussed a way to ensure we are praying God's will. What was that?

By praying God's promises back to Him, we can be assured He will answer those requests in His perfect timing.

## Praying Scripture for Yourself

Because it can be very hard to pray God's will for our own lives, let's use scripture prayers, like we did last week for others, to pray for ourselves. If you are in a group, start together with a time of praising God, then silent confession, and then rejoicing in God's blessings through a time of thanksgiving.

Before separating into smaller groups, review the scripture prayers together and then spend some quiet time alone with God, asking Him which verse He wants you to focus on in prayer today. Then break into groups of two or three. Each person takes a turn praying a verse for herself, with the other person(s) continuing in prayer on that topic, praying in one accord as we did in the last lesson. As you have time, continue taking turns praying additional scriptures. During the week you'll have extended time to pray these verses again for yourself.

### From John 15:5

Lord, You are the vine; I am a branch. Help me remain and abide in You so I will bear much fruit, because apart from You I can do nothing.

### From Psalm 16:8

Lord, help me keep my eyes always on You, so that with You at my right hand, I will not be shaken.

### From Ephesians 2:10

Lord, help me understand that I am Your handiwork, created in Christ Jesus to do good works, which You prepared in advance for me to do. Lord, help me not to miss the opportunities that You have planned for me to do.

### From Isaiah 41:10

Lord, help me to not fear, because I am with You. Help me to not be dismayed, for You are my God. Strengthen me, and help me, Lord. Uphold me with Your righteous right hand.

### From Philippians 4:6-7

Lord, help me to not be anxious about anything, but in every situation, by prayer and petition, with thanksgiving, may I present my requests to You, so that Your peace, which transcends all understanding, will guard my heart and mind in Christ Jesus.

# Personal Reflections

This week pray through the four steps of prayer. During your intercession time, start by praying the scripture for the person for whom you're praying. Then pray a petition prayer for yourself using a scripture prayer. The ones from this week's lesson have been included for you to pray with more focus. However, feel free to pray any verse God brings to mind. Afterward, draw an abstract or illustration of God answering that prayer. Release any concerns about artistic ability so you can allow God's truths to penetrate your mind and your heart.

A prayer on behalf of those pursuing a life unshaken in Christ:

> Lord, as we learn to bring all our cares to You, our loving heavenly Father, help us keep our eyes always on You so that with You at our right hand, we will not be shaken. Help us to remember we are each Your handiwork, created in Christ Jesus to do good works, which You prepared in advance for us to do. When we begin to feel anxious, help us remember to bring every request to You, with thanksgiving, so You will fill us with Your peace that is beyond all human understanding, and guard our hearts and minds in Christ Jesus. In Your sovereign name, amen.

## Day One

Write a prayer of praise.

Write a prayer of confession.

Write a prayer of thanksgiving.

Write a prayer of intercession for someone else.

Pray a prayer of petition for yourself, using the verse referenced below. Then draw a picture of what it will look like when God answers this prayer.

## John 15:5

Lord, You are the vine; I am a branch. Help me remain and abide in You so I will bear much fruit, because apart from You I can do nothing.

## Day Two

Write a prayer of praise.

Write a prayer of confession.

Write a prayer of thanksgiving.

Write a prayer of intercession for someone else.

Pray a prayer of petition for yourself, using the verse referenced below. Then draw a picture of what it will look like when God answers this prayer.

## Psalm 16:8

> Lord, help me keep my eyes always on You, so with You at my right hand, I will not be shaken.

## Day Three

Write a prayer of praise.

Write a prayer of confession.

Write a prayer of thanksgiving.

Write a prayer of intercession for someone else.

Pray a prayer of petition for yourself, using the verse referenced below. Then draw a picture of what it will look like when God answers this prayer.

## Ephesians 2:10

Lord, help me understand that I am Your handiwork, created in Christ Jesus to do good works, which You prepared in advance for me to do. Help me not to miss the opportunities You have planned for me.

# Day Four

Write a prayer of praise.

Write a prayer of confession.

Write a prayer of thanksgiving.

Write a prayer of intercession for someone else.

Pray a prayer of petition for yourself, using the verse referenced below. Then draw a picture of what it will look like when God answers this prayer.

## Isaiah 41:10

Lord, help me not to fear, because I am with You. Help me not be dismayed, for You are my God. Strengthen me, and help me. Please uphold me with Your righteous right hand.

## Day Five

Write a prayer of praise.

Write a prayer of confession.

Write a prayer of thanksgiving.

Write a prayer of intercession for someone else.

Pray a prayer of petition for yourself, using the verse referenced below. Then draw a picture of what it will look like when God answers this prayer.

## Philippians 4:6-7

Lord, help me not to be anxious about anything, but in every situation, by prayer and petition, with thanksgiving, may I present my requests to You, so that Your peace, which transcends all understanding, will guard my heart and mind in Christ Jesus.

# 8

# Turning Your Fears into Prayers

We can go throughout our days experiencing many emotions, feelings, and waves of fear and yet never take a moment to identify them, let alone pray to give God control of those emotions. Let's take time now to explore how we feel.

1.  How do you feel today? Create an emoji (emoticon) to express your emotion.

If you're in a group, share your emojis with others in your group, briefly explaining how you're feeling.

For this lesson, we'll talk about how to turn our fears into prayers. But first, we have to identify our fears. Sometimes fear is the underlying cause of feeling anxious, angry, agitated, worried, discouraged, disappointed, disgruntled, grumpy, and so on. And, boy, does Satan love to grab hold of those fears and help them fester and grow.

The key to stopping the infestation of negative emotions that grow when we take our eyes off Christ and onto a problem (or perceived problem) is taking those fears into God's light. The anxiety that grows with all the fearful "what-ifs" shakes us and eradicates our peace and joy.

2. Take a few minutes to quietly ask the Lord what fear might be constricting your heart. Then draw or write out that fear.

Now take that fear to the logical conclusion. For example, are you afraid your friend or child might get hurt playing football? Imagine that he did get hurt. What would happen next? Maybe he'd miss a few games, or maybe he'd be out the entire season—or maybe his whole football career would be finished and he wouldn't get a scholarship. And then what? Is it possible that God could use even the worst possible consequence to grow that person's character—and yours and others around you? Maybe it's through the injury that God will truly call that person to Himself or direct his path.

3. How do you think God could use even a scary diagnosis, horrifying accident, or failed class to draw someone closer to Him, or direct someone's path, or bring about the good He promises in Romans 8:28?

4. Being afraid is a normal human emotion. Yet read 1 John 4:18. "There is no fear in love. But perfect love drives out fear, because fear has to do with punishment. The one who fears is not made perfect in love." If we love Christ, we trust Him. How do you think trust and love go together?

5. Do you think your fear comes from not trusting that God loves you and your family and friends more than you could ever imagine, and that He has the *best* plan for all of you?

---

6. Illustrate 1 John 4:18 with God's perfect love driving out the fear in your own life. (Remember, stick figures are totally acceptable!)

7. What role do you think prayer has in chasing away your fear?

. . . . . . . . . . . . . . . . . . . . . . . . . . . .

Do you remember our discussion on 1 John 5:14-15? "This is the confidence we have in approaching God: that if we ask anything according to his will, he hears us. And if we know that he hears us—whatever we ask—we know that we have what we asked of him." Often, it's hard to give up our fears. We cling to our worries and anxieties as if it helps us hold on to the person we're worried about. But guess what! It doesn't. In fact, God tells us in 1 Peter 5:7, "Cast all your anxiety on him because he cares for you."

8. What's keeping you from allowing such confidence in Christ to chase away your fear?

. . . . . . . . . . . . . . . . . . . . . . . . . . . .

Let's look at Joshua in the Old Testament. If anyone had reason to fear, it was him. He was appointed as the next leader of the Israelites following Moses. *The Moses!* The one who was allowed a glimpse of God. The one who had personal conversations with God and who was given the Ten Commandments. Yes, *that* Moses! On top of that, Joshua's first assignment was to take the Israelites into the very land "flowing with milk and honey" they refused to go to 40 years earlier. Talk about fearful!

Read Joshua 1:6-9 and count how many times God tells Joshua to be strong or courageous or not to fear. Woven within the instructions is a lot of encouragement. In some Bible versions, Joshua 1:9 says, "Do not be terrified." The NASB says, "Do not tremble or be dismayed."

9. Now look at the very last section of verse 9. Why should we not be frightened or terrified or discouraged?

"The Lord your God will be _____."

This points us back to our main *Unshaken* verse: Psalm 16:8. "I keep my eyes always on the Lord. With him at my right hand, I will not be shaken." Our job is to keep our eyes on the Lord and place Him in His rightful place of honor. He is above all. As you do this you will not be shaken. Are you worried or frightened? Take Jesus' loving hand and keep your eyes on Him, and He will help you stand unshaken, no matter what crazy storm might be swirling around you.

Close today's lesson in a time of prayer. Start by focusing on the attributes that remind us not to be fearful: He is trustworthy, always with us, loving, and His perfect love casts out fear. Then have a time of silent confession, asking God to forgive you for the times you are fearful, worried, and anxious.

Now spend time thanking God for the answered prayers you have seen. Remember past times when you were fearful, but God swooped in and showed Himself faithful, trustworthy, and loving. Then, if you are in a group study, break into groups of twos or threes and pray for each other not to be fearful. Start with this scripture prayer for yourself, with one or two others praying alongside you in one-accord prayer.

### Joshua 1:9

Lord, You have commanded me to be strong and courageous. I need Your help to not be afraid or discouraged. Help me remember that You are with me wherever I go—and You are with my loved ones wherever they go.

Last, spend time turning your fears into prayers, following the command in 1 Peter 5:7 to give God all your worries and anxieties, knowing that He cares about you.

## Personal Reflections

Each day this week, start by reading Joshua 1:7-9. Reading the same scriptures for a few days at a time facilitates the meditation on that passage. Really let the scriptures be the marinade for your mind, washing away the fear and anxiety. Try to memorize Joshua 1:9 and hide this truth in your heart so you can meditate on it whenever you feel afraid or shaken.

A prayer on behalf of those pursuing a life unshaken in Christ:

> Lord, we praise You for being our strength and for hearing our prayers. When we feel fearful or anxious, help us release our fear and anxiety over to You, so You can replace our worry with Your inexplicable peace. Remind us that we do not need to be afraid or discouraged, because You are with us wherever we go. You tell us there is no fear in love, because perfect love drives out fear. We ask You to drive out the fear in our lives with Your powerful and sacrificial love for us. May we be able to stand unshaken because of Your love. In the power of Your name, amen.

## Day One

Read 1 John 4:7-18 and write a prayer of praise, based on an attribute of God found in this scripture.

Confess your fears and ask God's help in casting all your anxiety on Him (1 Peter 5:7).

Write a prayer of thanksgiving.

Pray using 1 John 4:18.

Lord, help me remember that there is no fear in love because Your perfect love drives out fear. Please drive out my fear.

Now spend time pouring out your heart to God, handing Him your fears and asking Him to replace your fears with the peace He promises in Philippians 4:6-7. You might find it helpful to illustrate through art (drawing, coloring, working with Play-Doh, and so on) the act of giving God your worries and accepting His peace. It can also be helpful to go through the physical motions of lifting your worries up to God in surrender, and then taking His peace and placing it on your heart or mind.

## Day Two

Read John 14:27 and write a prayer of praise, based on an attribute of God found in this scripture.

Confess your fears and ask God's help in casting all your anxiety on Him (1 Peter 5:7).

Write a prayer of thanksgiving.

Pray using John 14:27.

> Lord, You tell me, "Peace I leave with you; my peace I give you. I do not give to you as the world gives. Do not let your hearts be troubled and do not be afraid." Please help me embrace Your peace so that my heart will not be troubled or afraid.

Now spend time pouring out your heart to God, handing Him your fears and asking Him to replace your fears with the peace He promises in Philippians 4:6-7. If it's helpful, illustrate through art or actions giving God your worries and accepting His peace.

## Day Three

Read Deuteronomy 3:22-24 and write a prayer of praise, based on an attribute of God found in this scripture.

Confess your fears and ask God's help in casting all your anxiety on Him (1 Peter 5:7).

Write a prayer of thanksgiving.

Pray using Deuteronomy 3:23.

Lord, help me not to be afraid, knowing that You will fight for me.

Now spend time pouring out your heart to God, handing Him your fears and asking Him to replace your fears with the peace He promises in Philippians 4:6-7. If it's helpful, illustrate through art or action giving God your worries and accepting His peace.

# Day Four

Read 2 Chronicles 20:6 and write a prayer of praise, based on an attribute of God found in this scripture.

Confess your fears and ask God's help in casting all your anxiety on Him (1 Peter 5:7).

Write a prayer of thanksgiving.

Pray from 2 Chronicles 20:12, 15.

> Lord, I don't know what to do, but my eyes are on You. Help me not to be afraid or discouraged, because of this vast army of problems. Help me remember that the battle isn't mine; it's Yours.

Now spend time pouring out your heart to God, handing Him your fears and asking Him to replace your fears with the peace He promises in Philippians 4:6-7. If it's helpful, illustrate through art or actions giving God your worries and accepting His peace.

## Day Five

Read Joshua 1:7-9 and write a prayer of praise, based on an attribute of God found in this scripture.

Confess your fears and ask God's help in casting all your anxiety on Him (1 Peter 5:7).

Write a prayer of thanksgiving.

Pray from Joshua 1:9.

> Lord, You have commanded me to be strong and courageous. I need Your help to not be afraid or discouraged. Help me remember that You are with me wherever I go, and You are with my loved ones wherever they go.

Now spend time pouring out your heart to God, handing Him your fears and asking Him to replace your fears with the peace He promises in Philippians 4:6-7. If it's helpful, illustrate through art or actions giving God your worries and accepting His peace.

# 9

# Waiting on God's Perfect Timing

How did you do turning your fears into prayers last week? Did it become easier over the week to turn to God when your mind started to go to worry and anxious thoughts?

Sometimes God doesn't answer our prayer requests immediately because He's waiting for the time with the maximum impact.

1. Read Psalm 37:4. "Take delight in the Lord, and he will give you the desires of your heart." Compare this verse with John 15:7. How are these verses similar?

2. If we are abiding and delighting in the Lord, then He promises to give us the desires of our hearts. The result of abiding in Christ will change our desires. Yet even still, God doesn't promise a timeframe. In fact, sometimes we wait a *long* time for God's answers. Write or draw one prayer request where God has you waiting for an answer. For some it will be that prayer request that nags at your soul.

3. Meditate on Psalm 27:14. "Wait for the LORD; be strong and take heart and wait for the LORD." Now draw a picture of you being strong, taking heart and waiting for the Lord to answer that prayer request.

4. Do you have an example of how God's timing was better than the timeframe you wanted for a request? Maybe it was a loved one's salvation, a job change, a shift in schooling, a revived relationship, or the provision of a car or home. If you're going through this study on your own, write about that life example. If you're in a group, share this with others.

• • • • • • • • • • • • • • • • • • • • • • • • • • •

In a group, take turns reading Psalm 77 aloud, specifically looking at how the psalmist changed his attitude while he waited. Then discuss what he did to change his attitude.

His circumstances hadn't changed, but by remembering what God had done in the past, he could pen this hopeful verse in Psalm 77:19: "Your path led through the sea, your way through the mighty waters, though your footprints were not seen." When Moses and the Israelites came upon the Red Sea, they had no idea God was going to part it for them. Yet Moses trusted God, and in

God's perfect timing He parted the waters so the Israelites could pass on dry land. Then He returned the waters exactly when Pharaoh's men were in the sea. Just as we saw with Jehoshaphat in chapter 2, God provided miraculously in His perfect timing.

The Israelites had prayed for years upon years for God to rescue them from slavery. They didn't know the baby that Miriam put in the Nile River and that Pharaoh's daughter retrieved would grow up to be God's chosen one in answer to their prayer. They prayed and prayed, having no idea that God's timing would be more magnificent than imagined. God's path to answered prayer led through the mighty waters. Only God could do that. And God always waits on His perfect timing.

5. Think about your own long-term prayer request. Why do you think God might have you waiting?

6. Read Romans 12:12. "Be joyful in hope, patient in affliction, faithful in prayer." Now draw the scene of you in your waiting situation being joyful in hope, patient in affliction, and faithful in prayer.

7. If you're in a group, take turns reading Psalm 130.

Out of the depths I cry to you, Lord; Lord, hear my voice. Let your ears be attentive to my cry for mercy. If you, LORD, kept a record of sins, Lord, who could stand? But with you there is forgiveness, so that we can, with reverence, serve you. I wait for the LORD, my whole being waits, and in his word I put my hope. I wait for the Lord more than watchmen wait for the morning, more than watchmen wait for the morning. Israel, put your hope in the LORD, for with the LORD is unfailing love and with him is full redemption. He himself will redeem Israel from all their sins.

What do you think the psalmist was waiting for?

8. We are privileged to live in the church age and to know that Christ is the Messiah and that He came to earth, died for our sins, was raised from the dead, and, when we put our faith in Him, gives us the gift of the Holy Spirit. But imagine living before Christ came to earth. In Psalm 130, the psalmist is determined to wait with hope and faith for the coming Messiah.

Can you imagine waiting generation after generation for the coming Messiah?

How do you think the Israelites must have felt while they waited and waited with hope, faith, and expectation?

9. Now, if you're in a group, take turns reading Acts 2:22-33.

Fellow Israelites, listen to this: Jesus of Nazareth was a man accredited by God to you by miracles, wonders and signs, which God did among you through him, as you yourselves know. This man was handed over to you by God's deliberate plan and foreknowledge; and you, with the help of wicked men, put him to death by nailing him to the cross. But God raised him from the dead, freeing him from the agony of death, because it was impossible for death to keep its hold on him. David said about him:

> "I saw the Lord always before me.
> Because he is at my right hand,
> I will not be shaken.
> Therefore my heart is glad and my tongue rejoices;
> my body also will rest in hope,
> because you will not abandon me to the realm of the dead,
> you will not let your holy one see decay.
> You have made known to me the paths of life;
> you will fill me with joy in your presence."

Fellow Israelites, I can tell you confidently that the patriarch David died and was buried, and his tomb is here to this day. But he was a prophet and knew that God had promised him on oath that he would place one of his descendants on his throne. Seeing what was to come, he spoke of the resurrection of the Messiah, that he was not abandoned to the realm of the dead, nor did his body see decay. God has raised this Jesus to life, and we are all witnesses of it. Exalted to the right hand of God, he has received from the Father the promised Holy Spirit and has poured out what you now see and hear.

Peter uses Psalm 16 as a prophecy for Christ. He urges his fellow Israelites to put their faith in Christ, the long-expected Messiah. While thousands came to Christ, not everyone who heard Peter's message chose to believe. Some refused to accept that their waiting was over, that the Messiah had truly come. Pride and arrogance stood in the way of them accepting the answers to their long-standing prayers.

Have you had any answers to prayer that have been hard to accept because it wasn't the answer you wanted? If so, list a couple examples below.

..............................

Take time to pray and ask God if He has already answered a long-held request, yet you are having a hard time perceiving it. If this is true for you, confess and embrace God's answer to your prayer.

Now it's time to pray through the four steps of prayer: praise, confession, thanksgiving, and intercession. Whether in a group or by yourself, start by praising God for His perfect timing. Then spend time in silent confession, followed by a time of thanking God for answered prayers. Think back on the times God has answered long-time prayers, and be sure to thank Him for that.

Today, as you lift up your request to the Lord, pray specifically for your long-term request.

## Personal Reflections

Each day this week start by reading Psalm 130. With prompts, you will then pray through the four steps of prayer. It is incredible how this way of praying becomes so natural in such a short time. What a comfort it is to know that in any circumstance, you can first praise God and know that He is faithful. This first step will turn your heart to Him as you continue to pray and offer your life and your every need up to His care.

A prayer on behalf of those pursuing a life unshaken in Christ:

Lord, waiting can be so difficult. Help each one of us waiting for an answer to prayer. Help us persevere, and grant us unshakeable faith as we keep You as a priority in our lives and set our eyes on You, the author of our faith. As You tell us in Psalm 27:14, help each one of us to "wait for the LORD; be strong and take heart and wait for the LORD." When fear and anxiety grip our hearts, remind us that You are with us always. Help us to refocus our eyes on You through praise, confession, thanksgiving, and intercession, using Your scriptures to pray powerful, persevering prayers. Grant us Your strength each day. In Your perfect name, amen.

## Day One

Write a prayer of praise, based on an attribute of God found in Psalm 130.

Re-read Psalm 130:3-4 and write a prayer of confession.

Write a prayer of thanksgiving.

Pray from Psalm 130:5.

Lord, help me to wait for You, as my whole being waits. Help me put my hope in Your Word.

Now pray the same verse for someone who has a similar need:

Lord, help_____ to wait for You as her whole being waits. Help her put her hope in Your Word.

Focus on that prayer and a circumstance that requires great patience, and pour out your heart to God in prayer, being specific in your request.

## Day Two

Write a prayer of praise, based on a different attribute of God found in Psalm 130.

Re-read Psalm 130:3-4 and write a prayer of confession.

Write a prayer of thanksgiving. As the Bible instructs us to be thankful in all things, focus specifically on being thankful for the waiting period. Allow God to speak to your heart to show you how you can be thankful for this difficult situation.

Pray from Romans 12:12.

Lord, help me to be joyful in hope, patient in affliction, faithful in prayer.

Is someone else waiting on the same prayer to be answered? If so, pray the verse for them.

Lord, help _____ to be joyful in hope, patient in affliction, faithful in prayer.

Today, pray that during this waiting period, God will grow your prayer life and increase your joy, stamina, and perseverance. Pray the same for the others who are also waiting.

## Day Three

Write a prayer of praise, based on a different attribute of God found in Psalm 130.

Re-read Psalm 130:3-4 and write a prayer of confession.

Write a prayer of thanksgiving. As the Bible instructs us to be thankful in all things, focus specifically on being thankful for the waiting period. Allow God to speak to your heart to show you how you can be thankful for this difficult situation.

Pray from Psalm 27:14.

> Lord, help me to be strong and take heart and wait for You.

Now pray the same verse for someone in a similar situation:

> Lord, help_____ to be strong and take heart and wait for You.

Write a prayer, being specific in your request, so you can look back to see how God answered it.

## Day Four

Write a prayer of praise, based on a different attribute of God found in Psalm 130.

Re-read 130:3-4 and write a prayer of confession.

Write a prayer of thanksgiving. As the Bible instructs us to be thankful in all things, focus specifically on being thankful for the waiting period. Allow God to speak to your heart to show you how you can be thankful for this difficult situation.

Read Isaiah 26 and pray this from verses 3-4:

> Lord, You promise to keep in perfect peace anyone whose mind is steadfast on You and trusts You. Please help my mind be steadfast on You and to trust You, so You can keep me in perfect peace. And help _____ have a mind that is steadfast on You and trusts You, so You can keep _____ in perfect peace.

Continue praying, specifically asking the Lord to help you and your loved ones focus on your heavenly Father.

# *10*

## Unleashing God's Power to
## Do More Than We Can Imagine

During the past nine weeks, we have explored how we can stand unshaken, turning our eyes onto our heavenly Father.

1. What has been the most helpful for you when you face a difficulty?

2. When has it been the hardest to transform your thinking and cast your eyes on the Lord so you can remain unshaken?

3. Read Ephesians 3:20-21 from two or three different Bible versions. Check out the first section of the verse. How much will God do for us when we ask in His will?

4. God is able to do far more than what we ask or think or imagine! His desire is to give us the fullness of what we request. We may pray, "God, change my attitude," and He'll want to change our heart, mind, and soul along with our attitude! We may ask for one fish, and He'll give us a boatload of fish.

He's not just looking at you, but at those around you. He wants to have maximum impact for the answered prayer, which is why He sometimes answers our prayers so much slower than we expect. Sometimes it's through God's perfect timing that we receive the "more than all we ask or imagine" kind of answers.

According to whose power will your prayers be answered in ways that are far more than you could ever dream?

_____

And where is that power at work?

_____

Yes, God's power to answer our prayers in amazing ways is at work inside *us*, helping with the care of our hearts and souls.

5. Who gets the glory when God answers beyond what we imagine?

_____

Christ gets the glory in the church and in Christ Jesus. But for how long?

_____

Don't you love that Ephesians 3:20-21 ends, "throughout all generations, for ever and ever! Amen." No matter what's happening in our world, Christ's promises continue "for ever and ever." Christianity didn't begin dying off with baby boomers or Gen Xers or millennials. Our hope in Christ continues *throughout all* generations.

6. If you are in a group, share a testimony from your own life or from the book *Unshaken* about how God provided more than all was asked or imagined.

7. Think about your longstanding prayer request and then draw it.

8. Now turn that into a written prayer request. Be specific. When we pray with specifics, it can help us remember that the result is from our heavenly Father, answering in a way that is more than all we ask or imagine.

..............................

Today let's spend extended time praying for those *big* prayers, those faith-believing prayers only God can accomplish. Remember to pray with confidence. James 1:6 says, "When you ask, you must believe and not doubt, because the one who doubts is like a wave of the sea, blown and tossed by the wind."

As a big group, praise God for the attributes found in Ephesians 3:20-21.

For confession, review James 1:6 above. Spend time alone with God, silently confessing and asking Him to forgive you for the times you doubt, for the times you lack confidence that He will answer your prayers in ways that are truly "more than all you ask or imagine."

Staying in a big group, spend as much time as possible thanking God for the answers to prayer you've seen these past weeks. Using one-accord prayer, with one "thanks" at a time, thank the Lord for the big and little requests, remembering that as you do, you're also reminding yourself and others about God's faithfulness.

Then break into groups of two or three. First, use Ephesians 3:20-21 to pray specifically about your request, asking God to answer it in ways that are more than all you ask or imagine.

After intercession, spend time praying for yourself and each other that God will help you stand unshaken. From Psalm 16:8 pray, *Lord, help me keep my eyes always on You, because with You at my right hand, I will not be shaken.*

Before closing, take turns praying Ephesians 3:14-21 over each other.

> For this reason I kneel before the Father, from whom every family in heaven and on earth derives its name. I pray that out of his glorious riches he may strengthen you with power through his Spirit in your inner being, so that Christ may dwell in your hearts through faith. And I pray that you, being rooted and established in love, may have power, together with all the Lord's holy people, to grasp how wide and long and high and deep is the love of Christ, and to know this love that surpasses knowledge—that you may be filled to the measure of all the fullness of God. Now to him who is able to do immeasurably more than all we ask or imagine, according to his power that is at work within us, to him be glory in the church and in Christ Jesus throughout all generations, for ever and ever! Amen.

## Personal Reflections

Each day this week start your times of reflection and study by reading Ephesians 3:14-21. Meditate on the truths of this scripture and use it to help focus your prayer time. As much as possible, try to memorize Ephesians 3:20-21 so you can meditate on this scripture when you're feeling shaken. Close each day by lifting up a scripture prayer based on Psalm 16:8 to look to God daily and remain unshaken always and forever.

A prayer on behalf of all those pursuing a life unshaken in Christ:

O Lord, we praise You for Your love, wisdom, and faithfulness. Forgive us for the many times we take our eyes off You. Thank You for not requiring us to follow You in our own human powers but in Your strength, endurance, wisdom, and peace so we are sustained no matter what. We can trust that You will help us stand unshaken. Thank You! And, Lord, we pray for each woman who has completed this study. Bless her to overflowing. Help her as she strives to keep her eyes on You so she can stand unshaken. We pray Ephesians 3:16-21 over her, that out of Your glorious riches You will strengthen her inner being with power through Your spirit so Christ may dwell in her heart through faith. And we pray that she will be rooted and established in love so she may have power, together with all Your holy people, to grasp how wide and long and high and deep is the love of Christ, and to know this love that surpasses knowledge—that she may be filled to the measure of all the fullness of You, Father. May she know that You're able to do immeasurably more than all we ask or imagine, according to Your power that is at work within us.

To You be the glory in the church and in Christ Jesus throughout all generations, for ever and ever, amen!

## Day One

Read Ephesians 3:14-21 and write a prayer of praise, based on one of the attributes in that scripture.

Ask God to search your heart. What do you need to confess before God? Ask for His forgiveness and for His strength to help you stand unshaken in that area.

Write a prayer of thanksgiving. Be specific, and try not to repeat thanksgivings over the week. Try to focus on ways God has provided for you that are "more than all you ask or imagine."

Before you start intercession, ask God who needs prayer today. Quietly let Him bring someone to mind and pray Ephesians 3:14-21 for them, letting the Holy Spirit lead you in continuing to pray for that person.

Pray a scripture prayer from Psalm 16:8 so God will help you remain unshaken and encourage others to remain unshaken as well.

> Lord, help me keep my eyes always on You, because with You at my right hand, I will not be shaken. Help me to encourage others to keep their eyes on You so they can stand unshaken too.

## Day Two

Read Ephesians 3:14-21 and write a prayer of praise, based on a different attribute in that scripture.

Ask God to search your heart. What do you need to confess before God? Ask for His forgiveness and for His strength to stand unshaken in that area.

Write a prayer of thanksgiving. Be specific, and try not to repeat thanksgivings from yesterday. Try to focus on ways God has provided for you that are "more than all you ask or imagine."

Before you start intercession, ask God who needs prayer today. Quietly let him bring someone to mind and pray Ephesians 3:14-21 for them, letting the Holy Spirit lead you in continuing to pray for that person.

Pray a scripture prayer from Psalm 16:8 so God will help you remain unshaken and encourage others to remain unshaken as well.

Lord, help me keep my eyes always on You, because with You at my right hand, I will not be shaken. Help me to encourage others to keep their eyes on You so they can stand unshaken too.

# Day Three

Read Ephesians 3:14-21 and write a prayer of praise, based on a different attribute in that scripture.

Ask God to search your heart. What do you need to confess before God? Ask for His forgiveness and for His strength to stand unshaken in that area.

Write a prayer of thanksgiving. Be specific, and try not to repeat thanksgivings from yesterday. Try to focus on ways God has provided for you that are "more than all you ask or imagine."

Before you start intercession, ask God who needs prayer today. Quietly let Him bring someone to mind and pray Ephesians 3:14-21 for them, letting the Holy Spirit lead you in continuing to pray for that person.

Pray a scripture prayer from Psalm 16:8 so God will help you remain unshaken and encourage others to remain unshaken as well.

> Lord, help me keep my eyes always on You, because with You at my right hand, I will not be shaken. Help me to encourage others to keep their eyes on You so they can stand unshaken too.

## Day Four

Read Ephesians 3:14-21 and write a prayer of praise, based on a different attribute in that scripture.

Ask God to search your heart. What do you need to confess before God? Ask for His forgiveness and for His strength to stand unshaken in that area.

Write a prayer of thanksgiving. Be specific, and try not to repeat thanksgivings from yesterday. Try to focus on ways God has provided for you that are "more than all you ask or imagine."

Before you start intercession, ask God who needs prayer today. Quietly let him bring someone to mind and pray Ephesians 3:14-21 for them, letting the Holy Spirit lead you in continuing to pray for that person.

Pray a scripture prayer from Psalm 16:8 so God will help you remain unshaken and encourage others to remain unshaken as well.

> Lord, help me keep my eyes always on You, because with You at my right hand, I will not be shaken. Help me to encourage others to keep their eyes on You so they can stand unshaken too.

## Day Five

Read Ephesians 3:14-21 and write a prayer of praise, based on a different attribute in that scripture.

Ask God to search your heart. What do you need to confess before God? Ask for His forgiveness and for His strength to stand unshaken in that area.

Write a prayer of thanksgiving. Be specific, and try not to repeat thanksgivings from yesterday. Try to focus on ways God has provided for you that are "more than all you ask or imagine."

Before you start intercession, ask God who needs prayer today. Quietly let him bring someone to mind and pray Ephesians 3:14-21 for them, letting the Holy Spirit lead you in continuing to pray for that person.

Pray a scripture prayer from Psalm 16:8 so God will help you remain unshaken and encourage others to remain unshaken as well.

> Lord, help me keep my eyes always on You, because with You at my right hand, I will not be shaken. Help me to encourage others to keep their eyes on You so they can stand unshaken too.

# Our Prayer for You

Thank you for taking this journey with us! We pray that through this study you have learned to transform your thinking and set your eyes on Jesus Christ, the author and perfecter of our faith—no matter what craziness might come into your path.

This is our prayer for you.

Lord, we pray for the woman holding this book. Bless her as she begins to put the truths in this book and study into practice. Please help her set her heart and mind on things above, and not on things of the earth. Every morning, remind her to set You as the priority in her life, carving out a sweet time with You. Help her remember to give each and every one of her concerns over to You, trusting that You will work all things together for good and that You will answer her requests in ways that are truly more than all she asks or imagines.

Lord, transform her thinking. Remind her, when she begins to get anxious or worried, to begin to praise You and to immediately confess her sin of worry. Then help her dwell on all the amazing answers to prayer You have given before, so that when she begins to lift up her request, she will remember that nothing is impossible with You. Help her keep her eyes on You, knowing that with You at her right hand as her top priority, she will not be shaken.

In Your precious name, amen.

# Tips for Leading a Group

If you're leading a group through the *Unshaken* book and study guide, *thank you*! We pray God will bless you and each one in your group as you strive to live unshaken, like Christ. Below are some tips that might help you.

* If you're leading a group for this study, we suggest you encourage each member to read the book *Unshaken* along with the study guide. Each lesson in this study guide, 1 through 10, works in conjunction with the corresponding chapter in the book.

* It's important to establish the group as a safe place. You might want to provide a written pledge members can sign, promising that what is shared and prayed about in the group will not be disclosed outside the group. A sample agreement form is provided after this section so each group member can sign it.

* As the leader, be sure to review and pray through each lesson ahead of time, and plan to add brief stories about your own prayer life or a story from the *Unshaken* book to help bring the truths of the lesson to light.

* Have crayons or pencils in a variety of colors available during class. For the first lesson, you might consider making Play-Doh available as well.

* The study is written with Scripture from the New International Version, so you'll want to have at least one copy of an NIV Bible in an app or as a printed Bible for the fill-in-the-blank answers.

* We, Sally and Cyndie, have provided a prayer to start each lesson's week of reflections: a prayer on behalf of those pursuing life

unshaken in Christ. You might choose to pray that prayer over the women in the study to begin your time together.

* Consider using the provided introductory prayer mentioned above at the beginning of the lesson to help the women warm up to the practice of praying out loud. Ask two or three women to read the prayer aloud, each as though she is praying for the heart of every other woman in the group. Allow for a brief time of silence between readings so the words of unshaken encouragement can sink deep into the heart of everyone present.

* For lessons 2 through 10, start each one by referring to the previous week's lesson and allow time for members to share. Sometimes it helps if the leader starts by saying something like, "God really spoke to me this week as I meditated on..." or by asking, "What did God show you this week during your quiet time?"

* We've provided room to write answers to the open-ended questions. However, if you're going through the lesson as a group, don't wait for the members to write an answer. Use those questions to facilitate discussion.

* Embrace the quiet—once you ask a question, sit awhile and see if anyone will answer. Usually someone will break the silence.

* If your group consists of fewer than 12 people, feel free to call on each person for an answer so the members who are less vocal have an opportunity to share.

* Encourage each person to share her picture or answer. It helps if you're vulnerable and share yours, not from a place of "I have the answers" but from the aspect of "We're learning this together."

* When you talk about confession within the four steps of prayer, please encourage silent confession between each woman and God. We advise James 5:16, "Confess your sins to each other and pray for

each other," to take place with an accountability partner or trust-worthy friend outside of the group study time.

* Our suggested length of time for a study group is 60 to 90 minutes.

* If you have more than an hour, you can expand each section listed in the sample schedule, but also add time to model the prayer time before asking the groups to break up into twos or threes for inter-cession. This might be helpful if the majority of people are not familiar with the four steps of prayer and praying in one-accord, agreement prayer.

* If you have only one hour for the lesson, you might want to break it up like the sample given. Progressively give a little more time for prayer each week.

## Small Group Agreement

I, _____, agree to participate in this small group with love and respect for how God created each one of us with different strengths and weaknesses.

I agree to listen to the experiences of others without judging or offering advice, and I will bring each item of concern to the Lord in prayer.

I agree to hold in confidence all personal details that are shared or prayed in this group, and I promise not to disclose what others share and pray confidentially.

I agree to participate fully, allowing the Lord to gently draw me ever closer to Him as we learn to stand unshaken by keeping our eyes on the Lord.

NAME _____

DATE _____

## Sample Schedule for a Group Study

5 minutes

> Welcome
>
> Short ice-breaker question. Asking a fun, open-ended question or playing a simple, short game not only helps everyone in the group get to know each other better, but provides a warm-up for the discussion. It allows everyone to share out loud right away so they don't feel awkward the first time they answer a question that day.
>
> Examples: *What's your favorite vacation spot?* Or, *What was your favorite thing about kindergarten?*

5–10 minutes

> Ask about last week's personal reflections.
>
> Example: *Did God speak to you as you meditated on God's Word and prayed this week?*

20–35 minutes

> Read through the lesson, allowing time for the women to complete the answers, look up scripture, and draw or write the verses.

15–25 minutes

> Spend time praying as described in the Group Prayer Time section in this study guide. If you have additional time, continue praying for specific needs on each person's heart, using one-accord, agreement prayer (described in the following section).

# Group Prayer Time

Praying out loud connects our hearts with one another and with God. We know from experience that it can take time for some women to become comfortable speaking their prayers in a group. Here are some helps for your time of prayer.

- Please encourage *praying* the requests at the end, not *discussing* the requests. If time is of the essence, you can ask one person to pray aloud. We will provide you with prayer prompts for each lesson, but be sensitive to the needs of the group and allow the women time to pray for their requests as needed.

- Some people are not comfortable with praying out loud as God leads. Those new to praying out loud might feel so consumed with *when* to pray that they aren't able to pray along in their hearts while the others pray. To help those who are more timid, consider letting people occasionally pray, praise, and offer thanksgiving around a circle. This helps them become more comfortable with praying out loud.

- Encourage those new to praying out loud. Often they will feel particularly self-conscious about their prayers. For those completely new to praying, let them know it's okay to repeat praise attributes. If a woman wants to praise God for His faithfulness, for example, it's okay for another woman to do the same.

# Praying in One Accord

The description below of one-accord prayer is modified from content found in the book *Unshaken* within the chapter entitled: "Wielding the Secret Weapon of Intercession." We thought it would be helpful for you to have this here as well.

...............................

Praying alongside another person in one-accord, agreement prayer is powerful. In Matthew 18:19-20, Jesus says, "Truly I tell you that if two of you on earth agree about anything they ask for, it will be done for them by my Father in heaven. For where two or three gather in my name, there am I with them."

God wants us to be praying for this next generation, our families, our friends, our neighbors, our nation, and so on. But alone we can grow weary and lose heart. We need others to figuratively lift our hands; to pray alongside us in one-accord, Holy Spirit-directed prayers.

Victory is always waiting as one-accord prayer is poured out before the Lord. We have seen scared, heavy-burdened women transformed into women of courage and peace as they witnessed God answering the prayers of those who were praying alongside them for their children.

So how do we do this thing called one-accord prayer? How do we lift up one another's burdens in agreement prayer? We don't need to talk extensively about the problem. We just start praying. As my dear friend is praying for her wayward child, for example, I listen intently and agree with her in prayer. Then I allow the Holy Spirit to pray through me, often praying for details that hadn't been shared because I receive clarity from the Spirit. We both keep our prayers simple and on the same subject. We pray back and forth, carrying her burden to Jesus, until that subject is covered.

It's an incredible experience to pray with others in this way. You will experience God's faithfulness time after time, and you will witness many examples of women remaining unshaken in their circumstances because of the power of prayer.

# About Sally Burke

Sally Burke, president of Moms in Prayer International, grew up in Cocoa Beach, Florida. As a girl, she was fascinated with the space program and later became a space shuttle engineer. It wasn't until after she married and gave birth to her first two children that she and her husband came to faith in Christ and God began changing her priorities. Her introduction to Moms in Prayer International in 1990 was life-changing. As a young mom and a new believer, she discovered how faithfully God works in kids' lives in answer to prayer and the importance of the bond of sisterhood among praying moms. Compelled by joy, Sally began to share this hope with other moms.

God has led her step by step, first as a Moms in Prayer group leader and then as a Moms in Prayer area coordinator for her hometown, Temecula, California, where God raised up 60 new Moms in Prayer groups. She later became the regional coordinator for all of Riverside County and its 25 school districts with 700 schools and half a million students. In 2008 Sally "took on the world" for Moms in Prayer International as the director of field ministry, providing spiritual and strategic direction to the ministry worldwide. During her tenure, God doubled the number of nations where Moms in Prayer groups are found.

Today, in her role as president of Moms in Prayer International, Sally is carrying on the legacy begun over 30 years ago. She's a dynamic speaker and teacher who loves to encourage, equip, and empower women around the world in prayer. Sally has been interviewed on James Dobson's national radio program *Family Talk* as well as on *Today's Faith*, Calvary Chapel's national broadcast.

Sally and her husband, Ed, have four adult children—son Ryan married to Claire, daughter Ginae married to Garrett, son David married to Liz, and daughter Aubrie—and two grandchildren, Grant and Genevieve.

To contact Sally, email her at info@momsinprayer.org.

# About Cyndie Claypool de Neve

Cyndie Claypool de Neve, who has an M.A. in Counseling Psychology, had her first article published in a national church publication at age 12. At 18 she started working in a newsroom and has written nearly 1000 articles, columns, and in-depth feature stories. She was the main editor and coordinator for the book *When Moms Pray Together*, published by Tyndale House in 2009, and was interviewed on James Dobson's international radio program, *Family Talk*.

As the director of communications at Moms in Prayer International for five years, Cyndie started the ministry's social media presence and initiated the use of video storytelling. To encourage moms to be praying daily, Cyndie coordinated the creation of the daily scripture prayers emailed to thousands of women every weekday morning. Cyndie also oversaw the organization's name change from Moms In Touch International to its current name, Moms in Prayer International, and helped establish the church-wide day of prayer, Bless Our Schools Sunday.

Today, she works as the senior director of creative and technical services at Emmanuel Faith Community Church, with about 4500 people attending on the weekends. She leads a department of nine, including staff in communications, graphics, video, media, and IT.

Passionate about prayer and helping people find their God-given purpose, Cyndie enjoys teaching and has led many Bible studies, prayer groups, workshops, and Sunday school classes.

Cyndie and her husband, Marcel, live in Escondido, California, where they have two creative and entertaining children—Elliott, who is in college, and Zoe, who is in high school—and three adorable rescue dogs.

To contact Cyndie, visit www.cyndiedeneve.com.

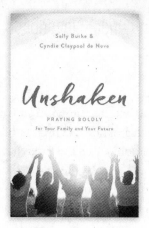

Your Faith Will Stand Unshaken

When Your Prayers Shake Up the World

As you pray to the God of the universe, you're free to ask for the seemingly impossible. Align your heart with His will and pray with confidence, knowing He will answer according to His perfect plans and with His mighty power.

Join authors Sally Burke, president of Moms in Prayer International, and Cyndie Claypool de Neve on a quest to pray boldly in your daily struggles and difficult trials. When your strength is in short supply and your courage is battered, it's time to...

- discover the power of a biblical four-step prayer process that defeats fear
- read stories of women who experienced answered prayer in desperate circumstances
- learn how to pray for yourself and your loved ones in accordance with God's will

Your family and future are in secure hands when you release them to Jesus. And as you pray with firm faith, you'll see yourself and your world transformed.

Want to stand unshaken alongside another mom,
praying for your children and their school?

Join a Moms in Prayer group today!
www.MomsInPrayer.org

To learn more about Harvest House books and
to read sample chapters, visit our website:

**www.harvesthousepublishers.com**

HARVEST HOUSE PUBLISHERS
EUGENE, OREGON